Who Rules the School?

poems chosen by

Paul Cookson

Illustrated by

David Parkins

MACMILLAN CHILDREN'S BOOKS

First published 1998
by Macmillan Children's Books
a division of Macmillan Publishers Ltd
25 Eccleston Place, London SW1W 9NF
and Basingstoke

Associated companies throughout the world

ISBN 0 330 35199 0

1 3 5 7 9 8 6 4 2

A CIP catalogue record for this book is available from the British Library.

Printed by Mackays of Chatham plc, Chatham, Kent.

Contents

Cross-Boss

Lollipop lady
takes some licking,
spends her time in
tick-tick-ticking
off us kids,
gives too much stick – in fact, of her, we're really sick – in
deed
we need
a sweeter
sort –
not a
bossy,
cross
escort.

Gina Douthwaite

Who Runs This School Anyway?

The secretary,
lab assistant,
groundsman
or the cook?

The new headteacher,
local preacher,
monitors or prefects,
bully-boots or swot?

The governors?
The government?
Captain Bligh
(the dread supply),
our dinner ladies
(straight from Hades),
our laboratory rat?

Pitch-markers, grass-cutters,
high-fliers, utter-nutters?
Parents or electors,
cleaners or inspectors?
Deputies, department heads,
exam-setters, go-getters,
County Hall or Westminster . . .
PRIME MINISTER? (Not *that*!)

Who Rules
the School?

Paul Cookson is married and lives in Retford. He spends most of his time explaining where Retford is. Dividing his time between looking after his son Sam and poetry he visits lots of schools performing his works and encouraging pupils and teachers to write their own poems. Paul is always polite to dinner ladies and secretaries. Mostly they are polite back to him.

PS: Retford is between Newark and Doncaster on the A1 by the way.

David Parkins has illustrated numerous books, ranging from Maths textbooks to *The Beano*. His picture books have been shortlisted for the Smarties Book Prize and the Kurt Maschler Award; and commended twice in the National Art Library Illustration Awards. He lives in Lincoln with his wife, three children and six cats.

Also available from Macmillan

'ERE WE GO!
Football Poems chosen by David Orme

YOU'LL NEVER WALK ALONE
More Football Poems chosen by David Orme

SNOGGERS
Slap 'n' Tickle Poems chosen by David Orme

NOTHING TASTES QUITE LIKE A GERBIL
and other vile verses chosen by David Orme

THE SECRET LIVES OF TEACHERS
Revealing Rhymes chosen by Brian Moses

PARENT-FREE ZONE
Poems About Parents and Other Problems
chosen by Brian Moses

TONGUE TWISTERS
AND TONSIL TWIZZLERS
chosen by Paul Cookson

The caretaker (true barbarian),
or our centenarian vegetarian ever-watchful ex-librarian . . .

They *all* have their say,
as far as I can see.
What this school needs
is just *one* boss . . .
I suggest

     ME!

Judith Nicholls

Pupil Power

Call on me if you need a leader
cos I'm cool, I'm no fool.
I could easily rule this school.

Tell the head to resign.
Take me instead and we'll do fine,
even though I'm only nine.
Under every desk we'll build our dens
where none'll be allowed but the under-tens.

Me, I'm cool. I'm no fool.
I could easily rule this school.

Make me the resident Primary president,
luxury lounge and private bathroom,
photo frames in every classroom.
I'll preside, unqualified,
over each teacher in the staffroom.
If they speak or make a sound
I'll hound them round the whole playground
till not a bit of litter can be found.

Me, I'm cool. I'm no fool.
I could easily rule this school.

Any pupil who sits still
will be sent home cos they're ill.
Break will be from ten till three,
with Cartoon Network on TV,
cans of cherryade given out free,
and chips and chewing gum on demand.
Sums and writing will *both* be banned.

Me, I'm cool. I'm no fool.
I could easily rule this school.

In the hall, for a treat,
bin your dinner of veg and meat,
and have a huge heap of sickly sweet
stuff that's bad for you to eat.

But elect me now or you're too late
cos kids from elsewhere think I'm great.
They know I'm cool; that I'm no fool.
They'll pay me to rule *their* school.

Nick Toczek

School Ghoul Rules

school.	year.	cries.	Hall.
ancient	every	and	ations
this	to	screams	Examin-
above	tight	for	The
high	clutching	listening	in
rules,	fear,	hypnotized,	all,
ghoul,	finger	I'm	us
ghostly,	icy-	if	for
ghastly,	with	as	wait
grisly,	grips	crawl,	dooms
A	It	I	Dreadful

👆 START

Mike Johnson

Mrs Clack, Caretaker

Mrs Clack *loves*
chairs on tables,
sand in tray,
bricks in boxes,
tidy clay,
lunchtime droppings
cleared away,
paint in pots
every day . . .

But when she finds
grey bits of clay
on the floor,
books all over,
paint on door,
sand on chairs,
an apple core
on Andrew's desk
and much, much more . . .

Then . . .
that's it!

She's awesome as
an albatross:
she snarls, she snaps,
she's crusty, cross;
she raves and rants
in loud dismay.

At half past three
things *have* to be
just so, *her* way . . .

for Mrs Clack's the boss!

Judith Nicholls

The Beast on Dinner Time Duty

The dinner line was single file
with no one allowed to speak,
and if you did you were sent to the back
of the line for the rest of the week.

She didn't like conkers or marbles
and playground footy was banned,
and if you were caught she'd take the ball
and burst it with one of her hands.

Everyone eats up their cabbage,
no one leaves anything green.
She's the Frankenstein of the food hall,
the King Kong of the canteen.

A beast on dinner time duty,
a roar that causes earthquakes.
Children shiver, teachers tremble
and even the Headmaster shakes.

A dinosaur in the dining room,
prehistoric, unfeasibly large.
Who rules the school? Don't be a fool!
She's the one that's in charge.

Paul Cookson

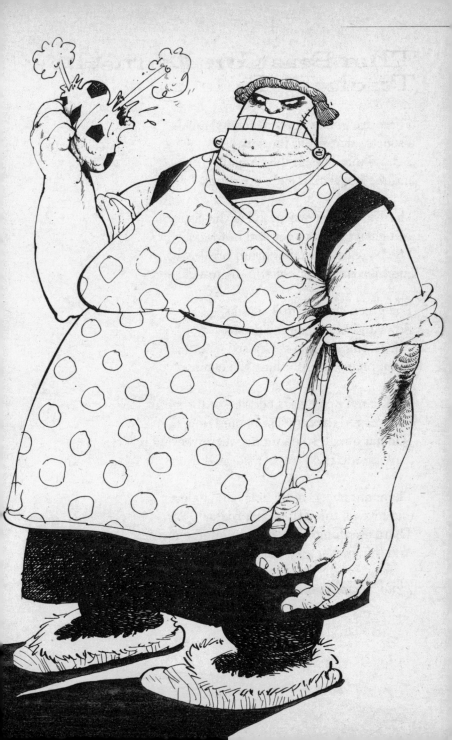

There are Ghosts in the Teachers' Toilets

There are ghosts in the teachers' toilets,
a spectre that sits in the sink,
a ghoul that lives in the plughole
and the bogeyman kicks up a stink.

There's a shriek of a spook in the cistern
as it chews toilet paper and howls.
The boggart eats toilet brush bristles
and bites great big holes in the towels.

The green ectoplasm it spasms,
glows and blocks up the drains,
a skeleton's stuck in the closet
and a phantom is flushing the chains.

Staff daren't pay visits because of the spirits,
cross legged they squirm behind doors.
The haunting's so daunting when wanting relief
they use the Headteacher's desk drawers.

There are ghosts in the teachers' toilets
that give all the staff such a fright.
There are things that go bump in the daytime.
And things that go trump in the night.

Paul Cookson

Miss Jones, Football Teacher

Miss Jones
    football teacher
red shellsuit
    flash boots.
She laughs
    as she dribbles,
shrieks 'GOAL!'
    when she
        shoots.

Miss Jones
    what a creature
pink lipstick
    shin-pads.
See there
    on the touchline
lines of
    drooling
        lads.

Miss Jones
    finest feature
long blonde hair
    – it's neat!
She 'bend' kicks
    and back-heels,
she's fast
    on her
        feet.

Miss Jones
        football teacher
told us, 'Don't
        give up!'
She made us
        train harder,
and we
        won the
                Cup!

Wes Magee

Night School

'Tu-whit tu-whoo. Who rules the school?'
Says an owl in the tree outside room three.
'I think it's me,' says the caretaker's cat,
Curled in the boiler room, sleek and fat.
'Me!' says a rat, gnawing at cables
In the floor space under the art room tables.
'Me?' says a mouse, all by himself
In the English storeroom – second shelf.
'Me,' says a cockroach on the kitchen floor,
Nibbling a chip wedged under the door.
'M-M-Me,' says a moth, bashing the light
That burns the entrance hall at night.
'It's us,' say woodlice on the toilet wall,
Scrabbling the plaster with its felt tip scrawl.
'Us,' say woodworm, slowly eating
Through the arms and legs of the staffroom seating.

Then comes the sighing, rustling noise
Of the ghosts of a thousand girls and boys,
Out of the ceilings, walls and floors,
Seeping through keyholes and under doors.
'We rule the school, you'd better agree.'
And all the other creatures flee.

Gus Grenfell

Dragon in the Library

There's a dragon in our Library
and she breathes fire
but only if you mess about,
talk loudly, complain a lot
and never read a book.

There's a dragon in our Library
and she has big claws
but only if you never listen,
annoy your classmates
or even, draw on books!

There's a dragon in our Library
and she has huge fangs
but only if you make a mess,
scribble on comics
and don't return books.

There's a dragon in our Library
and she can be a laugh
but only if you're good
she'll swop silly jokes
tell stories, find a book.

There's a dragon in our Library
and she can be nice
but only if you ask
she'll help you with your homework
and give OK advice.

Christine Potter

Watch It!

I'm in charge today
Better not get in my way
I'll turn your hair from black to grey.

I'll shove your face into the clay.
Throw paste and glue around and spray
Paint all over you, OK?

Because I want to, that's what for.
Just you hear me scream and roar
Shout and rant, kick down the door
Yell so your poor head is sore
Then be sick across the floor
Or even in the paper drawer
Once or twice, maybe more
So what if I'm only four?

Sorry, Miss, what's that you say?
If I'm good then I can play
Outside with my mates? Hooray.

You can be in charge today.
But tomorrow is another day
And I'll be back again, OK?

David Harmer

Nurse Greenaway Understands

Wendy's wasp-sting,
Graeme's grazes,
Roisin's rash and
Sanjay's sneezes,

take them to Nurse Greenaway,
to soothe and smooth and clean away.

Bottles, ointments, sticky plasters,
ready for the worst disasters,
yet she rarely uses these,
on throbbing thumbs
or bloody knees.

Gentle words, with healing hands,
are Nurse G's kit. She understands.

Trisha's toothache,
Nichelle's nose,
Benjie's boil and
Tommy's toes,

take them to Nurse Greenaway;
to soothe and smooth. She's seen a way,

but listens to each sobbing voice
and then explains her calming choice.
In Room A12 she's Queen, I'd say.
Yes, we all love
Nurse Greenaway.

Gentle words, with healing hands,
are Nurse G's kit. She understands.

Liz's split lip,
Tariq's thigh,
Eddie's ear and
Bab's black eye!

Take them to Nurse Greenaway,
to soothe and smooth and clean away.

Mike Johnson

The School Ghost

I moved the teacher's book
I threw her hat in the bin
When the sticky buns were really stuck
I put the concrete in!

I hid the cleaner's mop
I poured the milk away
I dropped the key on the cupboard top
Last Teacher Training day!

You can hear me cackle
in the middle of the night
when the school is lit
by the pale moonlight.
You can see my shadow
in the middle of the hall
when the school is shut
and no one's
                    there
                 at
              all . . .

I made the crayons break
I made the fire bell ring
I'm behind your last mistake
I'm the next wrong note you'll sing!

Things crash and fall and tumble
As I move through the school!
Walls and biscuits crumble
And the Head falls off her stool!

You can hear me cackle
in the middle of the night
when the school is lit
by the pale moonlight.
You can see my shadow
in the middle of the hall
when the school is shut
and no one's
                there
                    at
                        all . . .

Ian McMillan

The New Computerized Timetable

Science will be in the Art Room.
Art in History.
History in Maths.
And Maths in the swimming pool.

The lunch hour is from one o'clock to half-past,
Afternoon break has been moved to the morning.
Friday's timetable will operate
On alternate Thursdays.
Wednesday afternoon will be on Tuesday
Straight after Thursday's assembly.

From now on
We sit on desks
Write on chairs
And only wear hymn books when it's raining.

Next . . .
The new fire drill.

John Coldwell

Incy Wincy

Incy Wincy Spider,
By the classroom sink,
Scared all the children
Who came to get a drink.

Incy Wincy Spider,
Lurking in the drawer,
When the teacher opened it
She fainted on the floor.

Incy Wincy Spider,
Jumped down on the Head,
Now he's hiding in his cupboard,
'I won't come out,' he said.

Incy saw inspectors,
Writing their report,
Climbed up inside their trousers –
They cut their visit short.

Incy Wincy Spider,
In the teachers' loo,
They're too scared to go in there,
What can they do?

Ena cleaned the corner,
Where Incy's cobweb hangs,
Got bitten on the backside
By Incy's monstrous fangs.

Incy Wincy Spider,
Has only got one rule,
We all must remember,
A SPIDER RUNS THIS SCHOOL!

David Orme

Boss in Boots

If I ruled the school
every day would be the last day of term.
Every lesson would contain what you most wished to learn.
Every match that was played would be a win for both teams.
Every picture that was painted would fulfil all your dreams.
Every exam that you took would get one hundred per cent.
Every essay that you wrote would win the Booker Event.
Every meal that you ate would be superb haute cuisine.
Every model that you made would be a working machine.
Every term would be short, every holiday would be long.
Every child would be taught that all cruelty is wrong.
If I ruled the school that's how it would be,
but I can't make the rules for who'd listen to me,
I'm only the school cat but that's all right by me!

Janis Priestley

I'm the One Who Rules the School

I don't want to mislead you,
I couldn't tell a lie,
But do you know who rules the school?
'Tis I, 'tis I, 'tis I.

Without me kids would struggle,
And teachers couldn't cope.
Education officers
Would blindly guess and grope.

The secretary would resign,
The Head would go insane,
The caretaker would lose his job –
Cos I'm the modern 'brain'.

I'm the one who says what's what,
I'm the senior tutor.
I'm the one who rules the school –
I'm the school COMPUTER!

Clive Webster

GET BACK
TO WORK

The Scroll

Down, deep in a dark drawer,
    quietly closeted in an encrusted cabinet,
      secretly secreted, safe from sight,

hidden beneath the boiler-house
    and prepared for bloody letters
      is a scroll of scraped skin.

In fresh, fiery, fiendish letters;
    bright, bloody, bright-
red, riotously rich letters;
warm, wild, whispering letters.
In letters scrawled in bright,
    hot, wet, arterial blood.

'I hereby sell my soul
    and all hopes of heaven
      in the hereafter
        for the following:

windows that shut
and open again;

radiators that get hot
when it is cold;

toilets that never block
    and flood the school,
      however many paper
        towels are thrust
into the U-bend.

signed,
Jennifer Fogg,
headteacher.'

And in the doorway,
   the caretaker
      adjusts his horns
         and tail,
           smiling.

I.R. Eric Petrie

The Rules That Rule the School

Only speak when you're spoken to.
Don't stand and grin like a fool.
Pay attention or risk a detention.
We're the rules that rule the school.

Hands must not be in pockets
When addressing a member of staff.
Though smiling is sometimes permitted,
You need written permission to laugh.

Boys must stand to attention
And salute when they pass the Head.
Girls are expected to curtsey
And lower their eyes instead.

Sit up straight. Do as you're told,
If you want to come top of the class.
Bribes must be paid in cash
If you want to be sure to pass.

Don't breathe too loud in lessons.
Don't sweat too much in games.
Remember that teachers are human.
Don't ever call them names.

Only speak when you're spoken to.
Don't stand and grin like a fool.
Pay attention or risk a detention.
We're the rules that rule the school.

John Foster

The Unseen Queen

Doris cleans the tables
Polishes the floors
Picks up all the rubbish
Closes all the doors
Locks up every window
Turns off every light
Serves and makes refreshments
Every Open Night
Brews the tea for teachers
While the pupils play
Washes up the cups
And puts them all away
Nothing ever happens
When she's not involved
Running things like clockwork
Every problem solved
No one sees her very much
Behind every scene
But Doris rules our school
She's our Unseen Queen.

Paul Cookson

Mrs Thirkettle

Stiff as bristles on an old yard broom

There are —

Black as lonely midnight shadows

three hairs —

Long as a fisherman's lying fish

in the wart —

Thick as gravy left over from Sunday

on the cheek —

Bigger than the trees in the park

of Mrs. Thirkettle.

Can you go to the office,
      says the teacher
           – she knows.
And fetch some blue chalk?
      says the teacher
           – she's afraid.
Oh and can you get the register too?
      says the teacher
           – she knows the fear.

Iwillnotthink . . . !
Iwillnotthink . . . . . . !
Iwillnotthink . . . . !

(I will not think about the wart!)

too late –

Far too late.

I knock and march in

(Hairy wart)

I knock and march straight in

(Ugly hairy wart)

I will not think about the – shhh! nearly!

(Massive, big, ugly, hairy wart)

I knock and march in

(My heart in my socks)

I knock and march right in

(Pounding fear, awful panic)

I knock and march in

(I've never seen her eyes!)

I knock and march straight in

(never seen her lips!)

I knock and march in

(never seen her nose!)

I knock, march in,
and look her straight
in the wart.

I.R. Eric Petrie

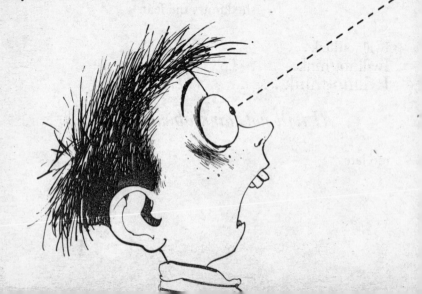

The Bug

A new bug
A flu bug
Has flown into town.
It's mite-size
But like flies
We're going down!

We've fevers
And sore heads,
We've aches and pains.
The classrooms
Are empty –
The flu bug REIGNS!

Sue Cowling

School Closed by Milkman with Measles

Frank the milkman didn't feel too good,
staggered to the bathroom,
gazed at his face in the mirror.
Measles! His face looked like
a dot-to-dot
almost filled in with red ink.
So Frank the milkman went back to bed,
and . . .

his milk float stayed in the garage
and . . .
the school caretaker's wife
never heard the clattering bottles
because there were no clattering bottles
and . . .
the school caretaker didn't wake up
because she heard no clattering bottles
because there were no clattering bottles
and . . .
the school caretaker didn't open up the school
and . . .
the Head had forgotten her key
because she had no milk in her tea
and she was grumpy and forgetful
and . . .
the Deputy had forgotten his key
because he had no milk in his tea
and he was grumpy and forgetful . . .

And . . .
Frank slept on with his spots
and . . .
a hundred children thanked him, lots!

Ian McMillan

The Bell

I am the bell.
I rule the school.

When I ring,
Classes snap to attention.
Anyone who ignores me
Risks a detention.

When I ring,
Latecomers start running.
Teachers put down their coffee cups
And sigh.
Playground games stop.
Children line up.

I am the bell.
I carve the day into chunks.
I summon everyone to assembly
And decide when it's time for dinner.

I'm in control.
Everyone listens to me.
With my shrill voice,
I can empty the playground
And the staffroom.

In an emergency,
I can clear the whole school
In less than three minutes.

I am the bell.
I rule the school.

John Foster

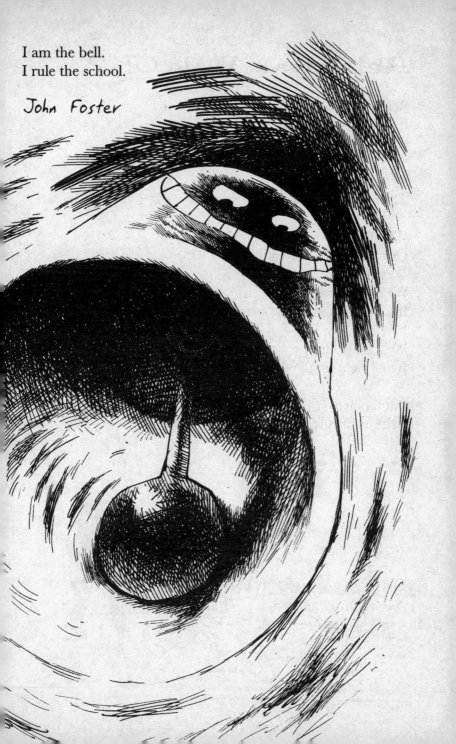

Rehearsals Rule OK?

Rehearsals rule – OK?
If you want a concert
Or a Christmas play.

We'll invite
The local Senior Citizens,

We'll delight
Our families and friends,

We don't mind
If we miss most of our lessons,

We'll make sure
It's all right on the day

But till then
Rehearsals rule – OK?

Sue Cowling

Time

My name is time. I rule the school.
I'm there each second of the day.
It doesn't matter what you want –
you have to do the things I say.

I tell you when assembly starts.
I tell you when the lesson ends.
I tell you when you go to eat
and when you're free to play with friends.

I handcuff teachers to the class.
The bell rings out when I dictate.
Sometimes I hardly move at all.
The term ends on the day I state.

When there's too much or not enough
of me for things you have to do,
you're cross. But I make all things end –
sometimes I am your best friend too.

Charles Thomson

Who Rules the School?

I, said the Head, like a fussy old hen,
I, said the Teacher, with my red pen,
I, said the Caretaker, cos I have the keys,
I, said the Cleaner, down on my knees,
I, said the Dinner Lady, sloshing out mince,
I, said a Governor, with pounds and pence,
Us, say the Government, with our curricula,
I, said the Nurse, with hands that tickle yer,
I, said the Computer, with all my data,
I, said Detention, I can keep you in later,
Us, said Exams, we test you and try you,
I, said the Radiator, can freeze you or fry you.

Who rules school? The wind, the rain,
and term time coming round again.

Matt Simpson

Ruler Rules

War broke out when Fountain Pen
Told Biro, 'I remember when
Your ballpoint tip did not exist.
Disposable! You'll not be missed.'

Black-lead Pencil, sharp and slink,
Pointed out, 'You don't need ink
To teach a child to draw and write.
School would close without graphite!'

Eraser squealed, 'You're just a fool.
I'm the leader of this school!
If you want to fight and shout,
Make no mistake, I'll rub you out.'

Notepad couldn't let this pass,
'Without me there'd be no class.'
Crayons, Felt-tips, pots of Glue,
Battled out their points of view.

Pencils speared across the room.
Tissue crumpled to its doom.
Binders formed a barricade.
Scissors marched out on parade.

Drawing Pins joined Rubber Bands,
Catapulting their demands.
Sheets of Paper didn't fret,
Origami – fighter jet.

Then clever little Paper Clip
Cried, 'Hey! You lot. Get a grip.
Gather round and make a pact.
We need a ruler, that's a fact.'

Straight and rigid to the law
Ruler measured up the score.
Inched himself onto his end,
Stood up tall. He did not bend.

Pam Wells

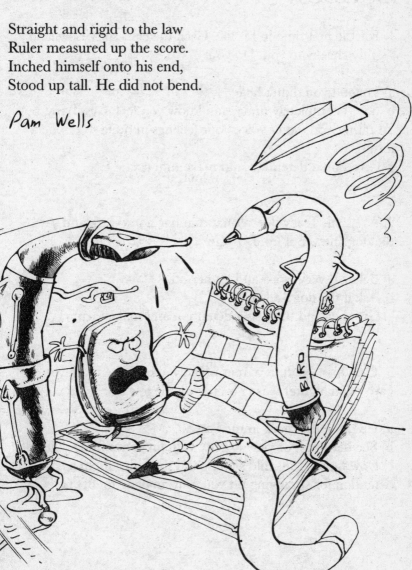

You Are The Teacher - Can You Rule This School?

1. For the first time in his life, Cecil the class softy is ever so slightly cheeky to you. Do you:

a) Pretend you didn't hear.
b) Say 'I completely understand how you feel, Cess baby, but I'd rather you didn't voice your feelings in quite so public a forum.'
c) Give him a detention and make him cry.

2. As usual, Tracy doesn't hand in her homework and says the dog chewed it up. Do you:

a) Believe every word and let her off.
b) Ask if the dog's all right.
c) Give her and the dog a detention and make them cry.

3. On Open Night a parent politely asks if 'the mark you gave my daughter wasn't a little on the low side?' Do you:

a) Upgrade the mark immediately.
b) See her point of view exactly without committing yourself.
c) Downgrade the child's mark and then give them a detention for spragging on you, thus making them cry.

4. You are on yard duty and see Big Baz bashing Little Lawrence. Do you:

a) Hide.
b) Say 'Hey guys, enough. Let's do some Drama to shake out those negative vibes.'
c) Join in and then give them both detention, making them cry.

5. A dinner lady offers you double chips and then double jam roly-poly pudding in front of all the pupils. Do you:

a) Say 'No thank you.'
b) Say 'Only if the pupils receive the same.'
c) Scoff the lot then guzzle loads more off the pupils' plates, making them cry.

6. You are teaching Maths and realize you can't do fractions. Do you:

a) Own up and apologize.
b) Say 'Hey, let's work this thing out together.'
c) Drop the fractions and dish out a really tough spelling test which all the pupils fail, thus making them cry.

7. In your assembly, a pupil makes a rude noise very loudly. Do you:

a) Ignore it, so all the school joins in to make louder ones.
b) Check it wasn't one of the teachers.
c) Give the whole school a detention, the teachers too. They all cry.

8. You discover one of your pupils tying up a supply teacher in a stock cupboard. Do you:

a) Run away before they tie you up.
b) Try to see this situation from both points of view, as they're tying you up.

c) Leave the supply teacher in there to teach him a lesson and make him cry.

9. In the staffroom a student is sitting in your seat, drinking your coffee from your mug. Do you:

a) Say 'How nice.'
b) Shake their hand and do some bonding.
c) Shout a lot, demand your coffee and seat back immediately and make the student cry.

If you answered mainly:
a) You should work at Mothercare.
b) You drive a 2CV, have a Greenpeace sticker, at least one earring and wear tartan Doc Martens.
c) You are on a par with Dracula, Captain Hook and Cruella De Ville. You can rule the school (but only when the dinner ladies aren't there).

David Harmer and Paul Cookson

SANDWICH POETS

All the very best from three performing poets –
sandwiched together in one tasty volume!

An Odd Kettle of Fish
Poems by John Rice, Pie Corbett and Brian Moses

Lost Property Box
Poems by Matt Simpson, Wes Magee and Peter Dixon

Elephant Dreams
Poems by Ian McMillan, David Harmer and
Paul Cookson

Tongue Twisters and Tonsil Twizzlers
poems chosen by Paul Cookson

Untwizzle your tongue unzip your lips
Untwist your tonsils get to grips
With rhyming rhythms for twisted tongues
Gonna rhyme those rhythms all day long
Gonna roll those rhythms rhyme those rocks
Gonna twist and tie your tongue in knots
Unroll your tongue turn up the watts
Unlock the locks on your voice box
Gonna shake your tonsils rattle your teeth
Roll vocal chords beyond belief
Twisted rhythms for rhyming tongues`
Gonna rhyme those rhythms right not wrong
Tongue twizzlers and tonsil twisters
Leave tongues sizzled and tonsils blistered.

Paul Cookson and David Harmer

A tremendously terrific and tantalizing tangle of poems
to tie your tongue in knots and tire out your tonsils!

A selected list of poetry books available from Macmillan

The prices shown below are correct at the time of going to press. However, Macmillan Publishers reserve the right to show new retail prices on covers which may differ from those previously advertised.

The Secret Lives of Teachers	0 330 34265 7
Revealing rhymes, chosen by Brian Moses	£3.50
'Ere we Go!	0 330 32986 3
Football poems, chosen by David Orme	£2.99
You'll Never Walk Alone	0 330 33787 4
More football poems, chosen by David Orme	£2.99
Nothing Tastes Quite Like a Gerbil	0 330 34632 6
And other vile verses, chosen by David Orme	£2.99
Custard Pie	0 330 33992 3
Poems that are jokes, chosen by Pie Corbett	£2.99
Parent-Free Zone	0 330 34554 0
Poems about parents, chosen by Brian Moses	£2.99
Tongue Twisters and Tonsil Twizzlers	0 330 34941 4
Poems chosen by Paul Cookson	£2.99

All Macmillan titles can be ordered at your local bookshop or are available by post from:

Book Service by Post
PO Box 29, Douglas, Isle of Man IM99 1BQ

Credit cards accepted. For details:
Telephone: 01624 675137
Fax: 01624 670923
E-mail: bookshop@enterprise.net

Free postage and packing in the UK.
Overseas customers: add £1 per book (paperback)
and £3 per book (hardback).